Daniel

Olwyn Harris

Reflections around the life of Daniel:
a prince who was forced into servitude,
yet still understood that The Lord was his defender

Suitable for Individual and Group Discussion

Copyright © Olwyn Harris 2025

ISBN Softcover 978-1-923021-28-0
      eBook   978-1-923021-29-7

All rights reserved. No part of this book may be reproduced or transmitted in any form or by any means, electronic, or mechanical, including photocopying, recording or by any information storage and retrieval system without the permission in writing by the copyright owner.

Unless otherwise stated Scriptures quoted here are from the King James Version (Authorised version). First published in 1611. Quoted from the KJV Classic Reference Bible, copyright 1983 by the Zondervan Corporation.

Published by: Reading Stones Publishing
Helen Brown & Wendy Wood
Woodwendy1982.wixsite.com/readingstones
Cover Design: Olwyn Harris. Some of the cover elements were created using AI Technology.

For more copies contact the publisher at:

Glenburnie
212 Glenburnie Road
ROB ROY NSW 2360
Mobile: 0422 577 663
Email: Readingstonespublishing@gmail.com

Acknowledgement:

My heartfelt appreciation to Pastor Dawn Peel, emeritus, who has held a role supporting the credentialling of pastors within the Australian Christian Churches Movement. Thank you for your willingness to cast your theological eye over these chapters.

Table of Contents

Daniel

Introduction	7
A New Beginning	9
Standing Tall	26
Bowing Low	41
Numbered Weighed and Measured	54
Sitting with Lions	69
Go your way	84
End Notes:	103

Introduction

Taking time to reflect on the stories in the Bible, is something that we are encouraged to do in our walk with Jesus. I don't know anyone who would suggest this is not an important aspect of being a disciple of Jesus. Yet I have noticed, over and over, there is a widespread illiteracy regarding the stories in the Bible which I grew up with. I've also noticed that this unfamiliarity is not restricted to new Christians. I suspect we are more comfortable with the popular narratives on our TV streaming service, than the ones in our Bible.

The Holy Spirit, in his wisdom, has chosen the platform of storytelling as one way to communicate our spiritual relationship with him, packed with wisdom, truth, morality, and values. It is not the only way God speaks to us, yet so much practical wisdom can be distilled from these narratives. Our challenge is how to access these stories in a way that allows them to be understandable in a world that is so far removed from the times when these accounts occurred. This series on *Reflections in the Bible* is not intended to be an exercise in theological exegesis, rather to create an opportunity to explore some of these stories. It is an invitation to go on a journey of reflection around what is described. What can we distil from these life-stories that makes sense for us today? Some of these narratives may be familiar. Some of them may be forgotten. Some of them are hard to understand. This is an opportunity to take time to slow down, invite the Holy Spirit to whisper his insight as we explore some of the stories he has preserved for us.

This book is intended to be a reflective space to use alongside your Bible. Sometimes, even the act of opening the pages of our Bible can be a challenge. So, open up! Don't skip over the suggested passages marked as "Bible Readings". The scriptures tagged as "Bible Reference" are intended to bookmark passages, if you want to check them. Take hold of the opportunity to read or revisit God's Word. You are invited to use these pages as a place to scribble in margins; explore your own questions; and use reflective prompts to go a little deeper. My prayer is that it will be a springboard to explore the incredible love story of God, his great good news of redemption and His grace will draw you closer to who He is as our Good Father. I trust it moves each of us to appreciate more about our relationship with God, ourselves and life in community.

1

A New Beginning

This series of reflections on the life of Daniel, is about one the famous prophets of Israel during the time of their exile in Babylon. The account of Daniel sits within the "Prophetic" section of the Bible Library. Daniel has a reputation of being a man of integrity and courage. This is what you prophet Ezekiel says about Daniel:

Bible Reference
Ezekiel 14:14

In challenging the practice of idol worship, Ezekiel highlights three men in Scripture who were identified by the Holy Spirit as exemplary examples of right living. These three men were Noah, Daniel and Job, and they were exceptional because they lived against the tide of the predominant culture. Outstanding because, somehow, they were able... in spite of devastating circumstances, continue to live before God with great integrity and honour. This gave them incredible spiritual influence.

But what I hadn't noticed before is that Noah and Job were historical figures. But Daniel was Ezekiel's contemporary.
The prophet Ezekiel was also one of the exiles taken to Babylon.
They had been exiled together, captured from Jerusalem and deported to Babylon under Nebuchadnezzar – the emperor of the great Babylonian wave of conquests. For Daniel, as Ezekiel pens these words,

there was no opportunity for historical polishing of his character... it was happening in real time.

If we would like to inspire ourselves about how to continue towards great spiritual influence, despite what is going on around us... even in the face of devesting circumstances, then like Ezekiel, we can look to these characters to see how they stayed true during these challenges. With that in mind we are going to open the pages of the life of Daniel.

Some background...

The name Daniel means "The Lord is my Judge". Daniel lived up to his name. He always deferred to the Lord as the higher order; the one who he was accountable to; the one who sits over the kings and superiors who were so fickle with men's lives.

But let's remember that the Hebrew concept of a Judge is not based on a court-room model. This does not mean the Lord is my magistrate! The Hebrew word for judge is "Shophet". We have a whole book in the Bible, The Book of Judges, which tells the stories of the ancient Shophets... the great Judges of Israel. These men were anointed by God as deliverers and defenders of the Israelites, to fight for them and shield them from their oppressors. The first work of a shophet, or a judge, was as a defender of the people, deliverers... not to act as a supreme courtroom magistrate. Their secondary role was that they administered justice and exercised good governance.

When I was in Grade 5, I remember our teacher asking around the classroom about some was one of the scariest things we had experienced. Perhaps he was trying to stimulate some feeling into our creative writing...

I'm not sure of his motivation, but there were horrifying encounters with dogs and horses, and snakes. Then one girl, said she had been through cyclone Tracey.
In 1974, she was living in Darwin, had gone to bed on Christmas Eve... and during the night her whole world was literally turned upside down. She talked about not being able to forget the sound of storm and her house ripping apart around her.
I knew my uncle, aunt, and cousins were living in Darwin at this time... But there was something about my class-mate's story, and the look on her face that stuck with me. This wasn't just a news report, or family members I rarely met. She was sitting right across from me, in the same room.
On December 24, 1974, a small, developing easterly summer storm had initially appeared to pass clear of the region, but quickly gained intensity and then turned towards Darwin with a direct landfall over the city. It became a Category 3 cyclone and is the second-smallest tropical cyclone on record in terms of gale forced wind diameter.
Yet despite those stats, Tracy killed 71 people, caused $837 million AUD in damage, (which translates to about $6.7 billion AUD nowadays, it destroyed more than 70% of Darwin's buildings, including 80% of Darwin's residential housing. It left half the population of Darwin homeless and required the evacuation of over 30,000 people.
As my classmate testified... circumstances can suddenly change...
This can happen to us at any time. We face a storm that can suddenly changes everything. It might come in the form of a letter, or an email, or a phone call, or a conversation. It might a diagnosis, a breakup, or a work situation. And change does not necessarily follow a scheduled timetable... like a new year, a new financial year... or an anniversary. Storms can come out of the blue. We are going one way... and then suddenly life looks completely different... and not in a good way.

Daniel was a young man living one way... and then suddenly his life is irrevocably changed. His life is turned upside down. And yet, even now, we are still impressed by the nature, and character of Daniel. So, let's look at the beginning of the account where we meet Daniel in Scripture.

Bible Reading
Daniel 1:1-7

Taken Captive

Daniel's life is dramatically changed... through circumstances outside his control. The siege that reads as a short phrase in verse one, was actually a two-year ordeal of incredible suffering.

Famine means the city, is finally subdued and overtaken. Ten thousand Jews, starved and weak, were exported to a foreign land under an oppressive regime. Good people are caught up in this mess. This change was not what Daniel had been hoping for. He becomes a victim of war as a prisoner. He was not in King Nebuchadnezzar court by choice – he was pressed into service... as a slave. He is taken captive.

How can God take times of displacement and pain, and use them to promote capacity in my life?

Change and Pain

Exiled, displaced, suffering pain and loss... these are not things that would be on anyone's list of new experiences. Yet... it happened. And out of this catastrophic chaos, Daniel has to make a new beginning out of what his life used to be... and what it is now.

He once was a free, smart, intelligent wealthy, young man with a quick aptitude, good looking and godly. That is quite the array of qualities. And now he is a slave. Property. Removed and displaced. That is a lot of change.

Loss of Freedom

There was Loss of Freedom. Daniel goes from being a free man... a young man of privilege. He was from the social elite... the account indicates he was from either the royal family or Hebrew nobility.

He is from the royal line, a prince of Israel, yet now he is considered a disposable chattel... a belonging of the Babylonian Empire. If you are property, and your owner is King Nebuchadnezzar... if he didn't like you... he would toss you onto the heap. Life is suddenly very vulnerable and uncertain.

Loss of Identity

There was Loss of Identity: They took his name. They imposed a heathen identity. Names are not just a handle in this culture... it is a reflection of who you are... a prophetic statement of identity. They give him a name for what they want him to be: Belteshazzar: it means "Prince of Bel." Bel was the ruling god of the Babylonian pantheon... the high god of the Babylon deities. They wanted Daniel to belong to Bel... Belteshazzar – Bel's prince.

Yet I notice that scripture acknowledges this as a legal name change... but not a spiritual one. Daniel never became a prince of any Babylonian god. Daniel continued to live under his Hebrew name... "The Lord is my Judge". Adonai is my Shophet. The Lord is my Defender. When his world was under attack... when everything was going pear-shaped, Daniel lived consistently with the awareness that The Lord is his Shophet... his defender... his deliverer. And he is still known by his Hebrew name, Daniel, to this day.

Loss of Hopes & Dreams

There was also Loss of Hopes & Dreams. There is the possibility that Daniel was made a eunuch when he was taken into service of the king. We know there is no record of him being married... or having children. We know he was a slave in a time and place where castration of exiled slaves was common practice. King Hezekiah was told that some of descendants would one day be taken from Israel to serve in the palace of the king of Babylon as eunuchs:

Bible Reference
1 Kings 20:18

Daniel 1:3 indicates Daniel, and his friends were under the authority of the "chief eunuch" (ESV), a man named Ashpenaz.

This same verse indicates that these young men were specifically taken to serve the king, *in* his palace. Josephus records that Daniel was made a eunuch along with Shadrach, Meshach and Abednego.

To me, there is a strong case that the losses Daniel experienced were not just home, family, name and identity, but also his sexuality... We don't know for sure because it doesn't specifically state he was castrated to be made a eunuch... but... there is a strong possibility.

I once suggested this idea that Daniel was a eunuch to a pastor who was one of my bible college lecturers and she became very angry, cutting me down for considering it. For her, this changed the story so significantly... that in some way, it challenged her ideas of who Daniel was, and that was unacceptable to her.

Whereas, to me, it suggests another layer of the profound loss and the painful circumstances that Daniel was living with.

Everything about his identity was being challenged and changed. Not just one thing... but many, many things. This was massive.

And yet somehow... regardless of all these losses that were imposed on him, he had to find a new beginning.

Living out the Consequences of other's sin

Was Daniel exiled because of his sin? This Babylonian exile was prophesied as a consequence of Israel turning their back on their covenant with God. Was this punishment or payback for something Daniel did?

There is no doubt, as we read the laments of Jeremiah, that Jerusalem was suffering this invasion, and these events of exile came about because of Israel's stubborn rejection of God. But there is nothing in this story that suggests that Daniel was part of that cultural move away from God. The Holy Spirit identifies him as a righteous man... a man of incredible spiritual influence.

So, if that is the case, this means he is living out of the consequences of other people's actions. Other people's ungodly choices. He was living in that fall-out. This is not his fault, and yet, he still has to deal with what all of that means for him... and his life. So, what are the choices that Daniel makes to start to build a new beginning in this foreign land and foreign culture and foreign religion?

Bible Reading
Daniel 1:8-20

Exclusions from the Culture around him

Daniel is in this culture. He had no choice in this. Not his plan. Not his preference. But he is here none the less.
He is in a place that does not worship his God.
He is in a place that does not honour his spiritual practices.
He is in a place that uses people as disposable chattels. There are power-plays and corruption everywhere.
Perhaps some of this rings true to you...
Perhaps you find yourself in a place that does not worship God.
Perhaps you find yourself in a place that does not honour your spiritual practices.
Perhaps you find yourself in a place that climbs over others, uses them and then discards them.
Maybe you are aware of power-plays and corruption.
Yet somehow... God takes this all this pain and loss... and uses it to position Daniel in a remarkable place of influence.
And much of that is because Daniel makes an intentional choice that even if he is required to be IN the culture, he will not be OF the culture.

Different Choices

Daniel makes a choice to exclude himself from aspects of this lifestyle and culture that he was immersed in... not out of rejection of the people around him... but out of his respect and honour of God. He was fully immersed in an elite educational program of the most opulent world power.

They were extremely affluent because they took all the treasures, and the wealth of the people they conquered. There would have been a lot of tempting opportunities... to just relax and indulge a little. But Daniel didn't.

In what ways am I immersed in a culture but do not want that culture to get into me?

He refused to 'defile' himself, probably because the meat and wine had been offered to Bel and other idols and no doubt their menu conflicted with Israel's dietary laws. Another idea[i] is reflective of the traditions seen in influential educational institutions today. Toasts to their deities may have been made by students as part of their meal. So perhaps Daniel abstained to avoid the libations offered to idols while eating. Regardless of the cultural detail, he chose to be diligent in these matters.

Perhaps he had an understanding before his time, that his body is the true temple of God, not the ransacked shell in Jerusalem that had been stripped and burnt and overrun by the invasion of Nebuchadnezzar and his troupes.

Daniel makes a number of choices... that says... "Yes, I am in this culture... but this culture is not in me. I don't have to be part of that. I can make a different choice. I will risk being misunderstood and not liked. I will choose... to do what I can, to exclude myself from these practices that do not honour God."

In some things Daniel was not given a choice: he was dressed a certain way... and was groomed a certain way.... he was presented with a certain curriculum to learn. But he didn't become a Babylonian in his heart. He was in the culture of Babylonia... but he didn't allow the Babylonian culture to be *in* him.

I also notice Daniel was not obnoxious or heavy handed about his preferences. He tactfully approached those who had influence over him, to be allowed to restrict his diet according to his law. He continued his practice of praying and worshiping God three times a day.

Where do I need to hold exclusion zones to protect myself from becoming part of Babylonia?

What am I asked to invest and steward at the moment?

Am I doing that well? What could I do better?

Prays blessing, not curses

Daniel was taught Babylonian law and culture, and he studied those things. This was a full-blown study program of language, literature, culture, legal and political science... this is a university degree. Three years of intensive study. And at the end of this term, he is brought before the king for a panel of assessment and testing of his knowledge. This learning was taking hold of an opportunity to find a new place.... but he is doing it as one who understands God is his defender.

First, Daniel lives his life, from the awareness, that he is first a citizen of the Kingdom of God and not just a slave for the king of the Babylonian Empire. But he doesn't retreat from life, he engages fully by taking hold of this opportunity, and he did it whole heartedly. He didn't just pass... he passed with honours. He didn't just scrape through. He blitzed it. He aced it. Dux. Ten times better than the others. He learnt... not just to study... but to take hold of the opportunities God provides.

Jeremiah was also a prophet of God at this time. He stayed behind in Jerusalem after the siege, and he writes this rather unusual request:

Bible Reference
Jeremiah 29:7

That is what I would consider a difficult recommendation: Pray that your captures prosper? Pray that this heathen ungodly regime does well? Pray blessing instead of cursing?

Do you think it is unusual for God to give this directive?

It sounds surprisingly familiar, like what Jesus said...

Bible Reference
Luke 6:28

This same idea is echoed in what Paul wrote this to the Roman church:

Bible Reference
Romans 12:14

We know Daniel was a man who made prayer a daily discipline... and we know he took the writings of Jeremiah very seriously. So, when he was setting aside time to pray towards Jerusalem every day, he was also praying blessing over Babylon, "...because if it prospers, we too will prosper."

Where do I need to pray blessing instead of the inclination to curse?

Bible Reading
Daniel 2:1- 49

Excelled by Stewarding Capably

Daniel is a young man when this story happens. This account is early after his graduation from his Babylonian studies. But he has learnt to stewarding every opportunity... because God will use each one to create more opportunities of influence.
When his job was a student... he studied well.
When his job was an administrator... he administered well.
When his life was on the line... he advocated well.

Excelled by Growing capacity

Now Daniel has been rounded up... again. Again, he is subjected to the choices of other people outside his control... even without his knowledge. He had no idea what was going on... except... this is a crisis. All the academic and spiritual advisors in the kingdom are going to be mass murdered.

What is actually going on, is that Nebuchadnezzar is distressed, and he doesn't know how to handle that in any way other than to use this fickle power-play is to intimidate his advisors into giving him what he wants: an explanation of his distress.

But Daniel also understands that God is his defender. God is the one who reveals hidden things. God is bigger than the whims of erratic and irrational men. Again, Daniel uses wisdom and tact. He doesn't let his emotional panic rule in this moment, but he draws on the capacity that he has been developing and exercising with every small choice that he makes, to deal with this huge crisis. He draws on his reliance and understanding of the sovereignty, mercy and grace of God. He understands that the interpretation of dreams is a spiritual mystery... beyond the capacity of human understanding. He draws on his relationship with God who reveals mysteries. He draws on his learning in people-management. He draws on his friendship with his mates... and gets them praying.

Gives God the Credit

One of the things I admire about Daniel's character is that he always gives God the honour and respect before others, even when they don't understand or appreciate how any of this could be, from their own particular world view.

Bible Reference
Daniel 2:27-28

"There is a God!" Daniel goes about doing his work diligently... but does not claim the spotlight for his own promotion, credibility, acceptance or elevation. Instead, he uses this opportunity to point to God as the source of this incredible insight. Daniel is careful to make sure God gets the credit.

In 2018, Skittles secured a very exclusive advertising spot at the American Super Bowl's game. But they took a different approach...
While other advertisers spent big bucks, attempting to connect with the Super Bowl's diverse and vast audience, the Mars Company decided to produce a multi-million dollar commercial, but instead of showing the ad to the games more than 100 million viewers, they would show the commercial to only one single Skittles customer.
A high-school student from Los Angeles, California, Marcus Menendez, became the target market.
The company secured David Schwimmer, of 'Friends' fame, to star in the ad. They hired a CGI special effects team and produced a tailor-made ad for this one person.
No need to worry about the preferences of the masses. No need to hire focus groups to create a spot with the broadest possible reach.

They only had to catch the attention of one.
"Every other advertiser is going out there and showing their ad to 100 million people," explained Matt Montei, the vice president of the Mars confectionary company. "We want to be the one brand who has the most exclusive ad in Super Bowl history."
True to their word, the ad was shown to Marcus during the Super Bowl game. It has never been shown to another person. All the masses could do was watch Marcus enjoy the spot, tailor-made exclusively for his pleasure.
When I read about this... I was thinking... "Really? An audience of one? Why would this company spend millions of dollars... to produce a campaign for one teenager which no one else would ever see? How could that be a good investment and get the advertising attention that they would want?
But hey... I'm still talking about it, years later...

This made me think about Daniel... He was investing his whole life... everything he had, for the audience of one. His audience was God.

He wasn't trying to impress the king, or amaze his tutors, or astound his superiors.... God was his audience. His exclusive concern. His exceptional focus was targeted on God.
But we get to watch Daniel as he engaged with this one single audience with exceptional excellence... and his fame has gone viral.

And we are still talking about him, not just years later... but 2600 years later!

How can I consistently live with God as my audience?

Final Thoughts...

There is a reoccurring idea has been impressed on me, while reflecting on some of these stories of Daniel. And that is this: looking in from on the outside, using the usual template our culture evaluates things... Daniel's story looks every much like a failure. There was no eleventh-hour rescue. His country was besieged, ransacked, destroyed and taken over. Daniel lost his home, his name, his sexuality, his culture. Daniel was forced into labour under a foreign regime, as a victim of war. He went from a position of nobility, to being a captive and a slave. We usually look for inspiration in the stories that go the other way... a slave becomes the prince; not where the prince becomes a slave.

Yet, we see that Daniel is renown as one of the great heroes of the faith... who, through all this, he lived a victorious life. Our Scripture confirms that Daniel is a man recognised by God as one who lived rightly and exerted great spiritual influence. And he did this while experiencing great pain, displacement and loss, with a profound commitment to the things of God. The Babylonians renamed him Belteshazzar - Prince of Bel - yet he continued to identify as Daniel...

He knew what his name meant... that God alone is his judge. God is his Shophet, defender, deliverer! Even in a culture that would take so much by force... God was still defending him. Even in circumstances that that look so much like failure... God was still his shield and his strength.

In this way, Daniel's story becomes an incredible example of overcoming and victory. Daniel made choices to embrace a new beginning and to steward each opportunity presented to him capably. And each choice... each decision... built his capacity so that he excelled at the things he put his hand to. With each success... each completed opportunity... each miraculous intervention, Daniel deflected towards God all the honour and respect and worship that He is due.

Prayer:

Father God, I thank you that you have recorded these stories of Daniel for me to reflect on. I thank you that I have his example to inspire me. He was able to acknowledge the traumatic changes in his circumstances, extraordinary pain and displacement, and yet still do life well with You. There is so much in these stories that challenges me. I ask Holy Spirit, that you would help me to be a person who will, regardless of what is going on around me, regardless of the culture I am in, I will not allow that culture to indwell in me. I want to be a person set apart for Your purposes. Help me to tune my attention so I live my life to an audience of one... giving glory and honour and worship to you first.

2
Standing Tall

Where we have been...

We have opened the pages of the life of Daniel... to see what we can discover in this book that might inspire us on how to live well in our relationship with God, in spite of what is going on around us. Daniel was able to embark on a new beginning and forge a meaningful life... even after his world was ripped apart from the invasion from the Babylonian emperor, King Nebuchadnezzar.

Daniel's name means "The Lord is my Judge", and we were reminded that the Hebrew word for judge is "Shophet" – not a magistrate, but Judges were men who were anointed by God to deliver, defend and to fight and shield people from their oppressors. So even though... at first glance... it seems like God was not acting like Daniel's defender and deliverer... even here... even in Babylon, we see that this occurs.

And one example of that was when Nebuchadnezzar has a distressing dream, rounds up the wise men, including Daniel to execute them because they cannot tell him his dream.

But God gives Daniel the content of the dream and its interpretation, and the wise men are spared. The Lord is my defender.

Now we continue on as we find out what life looks like for these Jewish exiles living in a foreign culture.

I remember being at a Bible Study group one evening, a friend shared that she had just been given a diagnosis of cancer, and she was preparing to go away for treatment. This meant she would be isolated from her family and friends. That is a daunting circumstance to be confronted with, and not surprisingly, she was concerned how she would handle that. To encourage her, we went around the group and prayed for our friend... and spoke a word of encouragement as we felt led. And one of the people there, referred to a story out of Daniel.

"God can and will address this," he said. "He is able to do that. But even if he doesn't, our choice is not to bow our knee to the god of cancer and live in fear of that. Regardless of the outcome, God is with you through this fiery furnace experience."

What he spoke was really impacting for me as it put a very practical spin on the story that we are reflecting on today.

My friend was facing a fiery-furnace experience, looming large and intimidating. Afterwards, she shared she had not felt alone as she went through that experience. She chose not to bow her knee... and the outcome was that she was cleared with good health.

There are so many different sorts of fiery furnaces that we can face. Like my friend, it may be health...or it may be relationships, rejection, trauma, abuse, or natural disasters. At some point in our lives, we come up against a fiery furnace, and it may not always exclusively be because of our Christian faith... but it is our faith that can be the difference of how we navigate these experiences.

In this story, we look more closely at Daniel's three friends: Hananiah, Mishael and Azariah. (or as they were known by their Babylonian names Shadrach, Meshach, and Abednego). Although this story does not include Daniel specifically, it is a powerful example of God as our defender.

So where was Daniel during this account? We don't know because it is not stated... and of course there has been lots of speculation. Probably, one of the most plausible ideas, was that Daniel's high-level duties of the Empire, called him away so he wasn't present when this all went down. Let's read the account out of Daniel chapter 3.

Bible Reading
Daniel 3:1-12

God reveals to Daniel that the dream was about an enormous, dazzling statue, awesome in appearance... a statue that is described as having a head of gold, its chest and arms was made of silver, its belly and thighs of bronze, its legs of iron, its feet partly of iron and partly of baked clay.

Bible Reference
Daniel 2:31-33

Did you notice that in Chapter 2 Nebuchadnezzar has a very powerful dream where he sets about to execute all the wise men because they cannot tell him what his dream is...and then, in the very next Chapter, Nebuchadnezzar has built an enormous, dazzling statue... awesome in appearance... but made *completely* of gold. No silver, no bronze, no iron and clay.

We read how Daniel interpreted the dream to mean that Nebuchadnezzar was the head of gold, and after him would come a world-power of silver... and after them, a world power of bronze...

What do you think Nebuchadnezzar is saying by building a statue made completely of gold?

I'm wondering if Nebuchadnezzar's intent is simply this: I don't want to recognise my mortality. I don't want to just be the head of gold... but I want to be the chest and body and legs as well. I want to sustain that feeling of fearsome power and dominion I had when I dreamt my dream! I don't want to acknowledge that my privilege and power is limited. I want to be the whole statue... immortal, divine, all powerful. I want to be a god.

If Nebuchadnezzar becomes god... then he considers it appropriate that people worship him. And he sets about to make that happen.

But... Nebuchadnezzar is not a god... he is a man. A privileged man... but a man none the less. Nebuchadnezzar's statue is not a god...

It is a statue – metal and inanimate. An imposing and dazzling statue... nearly 30 metres of gold high and 3 metre thick. That is an impressive amount of gold in one place! But it is still a statue none the less.

Conviction at a Heart Level

Daniel's Jewish friends Shadrach, Meshach, and Abednego are given the edict that they are required to worship this statue. They respond with conviction.

Notice that Nebuchadnezzar didn't just build a gold statue to be worshipped as an idol... he also built an execution furnace to go with it.

He expected resistance; he expected that the people of other nations would not comply with his proclamation.

And he was prepared. This was a very effective form of intimidation. Yet for these men... to be the only three people of "every race, colour, and creed", to be the *only* ones who did not worship this idol, this shows a remarkable level of conviction. It was a conviction that was engaged deep at a heart level.

How do I measure how deep my convictions are?

What stops me from consistently outworking my convictions?

Like Daniel, these men had their lives ransacked. Their Hebrew names were also changed, giving allegiance to the Babylonian gods... specifically the moon-god *Aku*; and *Nabu* – the patron god of scribes, literacy, and wisdom.

It would be expected that as Shadrach, Meshach, and Abednego are immersed in the culture and religions of Babylon, that they would eventually adopt and adapt to the religion of their captors.

Yet this is not the case. This idea of faithfulness and fidelity to God was embedded in their heart. This is not just an academic acquiesce, but it was a deep knowing in their spirit of what was the best thing to do.

It reminds me of what the Sons of Korah wrote in Psalm 42...

Bible Reading
Psalm 42:1-8

Deep calls to deep. There is an awareness deep in their being, that God is their only living source

Conviction at a Mind Level

But more is needed if these men were to stay true to their conviction in the face of such intimidation. This not just a spiritual experience... but it is also their *life* experience. They know that if their head is not in the right space, they could not follow through on their convictions: What do they *think* about this directive?

Notice that they do not talk themselves out of this. They do not rationalise or make excuses. They are confronted with a very challenging position: Bow down and live... or to be true to the One Holy God... and die. Do you notice how binary our thinking can be? Either/Or. Yet these men were able to allow that there is a third option that was not presented: they could honour our powerful, merciful God... and live. They were just as convinced in their minds and their wills... as in their spirits.

Remember... these men are part of the Babylonian academic elite. They passed all their studies with excellence. They are intelligent and accomplished men of ability. They have been promoted above their peers because of their competence. This is not a mindless, idiotic notion... but a considered conviction. It not only sits deep within their spirit but also is congruent with what they know and understand about their God and their walk with Him. And now, they stand tall by their convictions.

Conviction at an Action Level

Yet still there is another level of conviction that is required for them to hold onto the ability to follow through. Not only did they need the spiritual conviction in their hearts; they also needed the knowledge of God to holds them firm. But now they have a choice as to what they are going to do with this: Will they follow through with their actions? What must they *do,* to be consistent with what they believe and know? They make a choice to stand tall... when everyone else... without exception, is bowing low. This is an action that had consequences:

Bible Reading
Daniel 3:13-18

Willing to... be Visible

The thing about standing tall when everyone else is bowing low, is that you are going to stand out. They had to be willing to be visible.

This is not a decision they could make under the radar. Three men standing tall when others are bowing low is a bold statement. This is a very visible decision that they made.

Willing to... be Unpopular

They had to be willing to be unpopular. What I notice is that they are already unpopular. We are told that there was a group of people who were jealous of their accomplishments and wanted to bring the Jews into disrepute before the King. These three men were subject to those prejudices. Their stand brings them in direct confrontation with the system and those who were willing to use it to make an example of them. To this point in the story, Shadrach, Meshach, and Abednego had held a level of favour with King Nebuchadnezzar.

They were promoted by decree after Daniel interpreted his dream. They were favoured because of Daniel's influence. But now they stand before the Emperor himself and say... "We don't need to defend ourselves before you in this matter."

I *don't* read this with a tone of arrogance or conceit... but with a confident, yet humble attitude...

Bible Reference
Daniel 3:17-18

Willing to... bear the results

What are the consequences they can expect?

God is able. He can. But *even if* he doesn't save them, their decision was that they would still hold true to their conviction, even when it is different to every other person in the Babylonian province where this statue was erected. These men were not the only Jews captured from Jerusalem. They were not the only noblemen groomed and educated for the Babylonian court. Yet they were the only ones present who were willing to bear the results of this bold decision.

Bible Reading
Daniel 3:19-30

God's mercy and grace

They were able to stay standing by acknowledging God's Grace. Hananiah, Mishael and Azariah relied on God's mercy... but they were still subject to the whims and actions of those over them. They acknowledged God's mercy... but they still were sentenced to death, tied up and thrown into the furnace to be executed.

When things go belly-up... am I able to acknowledge God's grace and sovereignty... even when I don't understand?

They acknowledged God's mercy... even when the soldiers that carried out the execution were killed by the extreme heat of the furnace.

God's Sovereignty

So how do we understand this? Just as Shadrach, Meshach and Abednego did. God can... but he may not. God is willing... but he may not. Not because God is another form of a fickle ruler who plays flippantly with the lives of his subjects... but because he is God, and he sees the beginning from the end. He sees the start to the finish. He sees the detail and the bigger picture... and He holds every decision in love, with all of that detail in his sovereign hands.

There will be things that we do not understand. There are some things that we *will* not get our head around. Shadrach, Meshach and Abednego had their lives spared... and yet we know enough of history to know that there are many, many faithful followers of God who have fallen under the same conviction and made the same choice... and have been martyred for their faith.

There are times when we also have to rely on the sovereignty of God and say... *"God, I don't understand... but I trust you... and I am going to choose to believe this is a decision that is above my paygrade"*. You are God. You are sovereign. You are also love. That is my conviction. That is what I stand by.

God's presence

There are circumstances where we don't have access to some choices. There are circumstances that are outside our control. But there is something that God has ensured that we *always* have the choice about... and that is in the way we respond. Shadrach, Meshach and Abednego stood so firmly in *that* choice. That choice could not be taken away from them. They had a choice to stand tall... even when it meant they stood out... and they took it.

What is it like to acknowledge that I always have a choice... to honour and respect God regardless of what others choose?

Did you notice that they still were subjected to the fire? They were not rescued from going through the fire. Angels didn't come and put the fire out. Angels didn't come and sweep them up in their arms and whisk them away. But as they went through the ordeal, God was with them, and they were not destroyed by it. That's the bold encouragement of this story: they were given the strength and courage and comfort of the fourth person who was with them in the fire as they stood by what they believed was right.

Nebuchadnezzar declared that the fourth person walking around in the fire *looked like* a son of the gods. We believe he was *The* Son of God! They had the presence of Jesus with them in the furnace. When it seemed impossible to continue... they found that they were still standing up.

But... they were not just standing up... they were walking around! Think about that.... they were thrown, in bound and tied up ... Now they are walking around... freely!

The fire that was intended to destroy them, was used to release them, unbind them, and allow them to walk free... in greater liberty.

The fire burnt off their ropes! What was purposed to harm... actually released them. This is the greatest story of not just getting by but navigating through pain with dignity, and coming out in a better place. Only God can do that.

What is it like to picture Jesus standing with me in the fire ... knowing he is using what was designed for my destruction to release me to stand and stay strong?

He can transform an experience by his presence, so that we come through the fire more free, more alive, more aware of God with us. God with us... in the furnace... means we don't just stay standing up. We get to walk around freely with Jesus!

Louise Halling[ii] is a lady who lives with muscular dystrophy. She shares a story of the last time she attempted to travel by herself on the London Tube – on crutches with a large rucksack. She found herself at Putney station facing an enormous flight of stairs. There was no lift, or escalator, and she remembers standing at the bottom of these stairs thinking, "I can't do this. I just can't." She wanted to cry because she felt should've been able to manage the stairs, like everyone else, but just couldn't. She stood there and just prayed.

Then she describes how a man with the most amazing face appeared at her side. "Can I carry your bag and help you up the stairs?" he asked. She couldn't stop staring at him.

He took her bag, took her arm, helped her to the top of the flight of stairs, handed back her bag. And by the time she got sorted and turned around to thank him, he was gone.

She said, he was "totally gone!" Nowhere to be seen. She feels very certain her helper was an angel. I would understand her story in the same way.

Final Thoughts...

The happy ending to this story is the honour that this brought God. What had started out as a plot to sabotage these men, slander their character and their successes... ended up as a royal decree that *no* one could bad-mouth the God of the Hebrews. Their plot to expose them and eliminate them... ended up in them being promoted again.

I admit... there is a little satisfaction in that for me. But I also admit that it is a little weird for me at the same time – that they would be rescued from the fire and set free to serve and promote the wellbeing of their captors once more. God determined they could contribute good... in a place that really needed good people to be available to serve.

I also notice that, once more – intimidation and fear is the Babylonian modality to try and legislate morality: *"Don't you dare slander the God of Shadrach Meshach and Abednego... or I will raze your house to the ground and chop up your families."*

God on the other hand... our God is a God who will not use fear as a motivator. I'm not referring to the "fear of the Lord" – that healthy honouring respect... but whimpering and grovelling before the idea of a terrifying God with a big hell-fire, who is on a mission to catch us out and toss us in the furnace if we don't get it right. That is *not* an accurate picture of God.

Rather God uses love and grace and mercy and a desire to commune with his presence, to captivate our hearts with kindness; He wants the best for us, so that our minds, and our wills – are empowered to make choices that will translate into honourable action.

Our furnace-fires can come in many sorts of challenges. But we are not alone in them.

Whether we have the physical presence of Jesus manifested, or the presence of an angel, or the Holy Spirit within us giving us strength...a stranger... or a friend... God promises to provide us with what we need to get through our fires.

Bible Reference
Psalm 28:7

God is our defender: He is with us when we face furnace-fires. Sometimes we can cotton onto the idea that as Christians we should be exempt from all the challenges that other people experience. This is like saying our Christianity is spraying on spiritual ScotchGuard. That victory and living well, is actually being exempt from the struggle. Not getting thrown in the furnace to start with. But this is also not a picture that is consistent with scripture.

Story after story we see challenges and fallibilities and failure as well as overcoming and strengths and victories. There is no victory without the battle. There is no triumph without the challenge. There is no overcoming a storm if all we experience is smooth sailing. This was something that occurred for Shadrach, Meshach and Abednego.

They stood tall... they stood out... and yet they were able to continue to navigate through their situation with dignity and without compromise. As they stood with integrity, they *did* come against and confront those things that lacked integrity... in this case it was the edict to worship the statue of a heathen emperor.

As someone once observed, they didn't say, *'We're going to trust in God because He is going to deliver us from the fire."*
They said, *'We're going to trust in God even if He decides not to deliver us.'*

As they stood tall, holding a light they *did* come against and confront those things that represented darkness. These three men went from a position of favour in the Empire... to being condemned to death because they held tight to a conviction and followed-through in their faithfulness to God regardless.

God in his sovereignty – turned that around for good. They not only survived the fire, but they were also given even more opportunities to contribute good through their service in the future. They believed God would rescue them but allowed that even if he didn't... they would choose to honour God anyway.

Prayer:

Father God, I thank you that you see me. I thank you that you know the challenges that I face each day. Even when I am confronted with fiery furnaces, Holy Spirit, help me to be a person of conviction. Help me to stand tall and not bow to the pressure to be like those around me. Help me to be faithful to You and Your name. I do not want to be a person who would be intimidated and cower in the face of those things that would come against Your glory and honour. Thank You for the encouragement You offer in this story, that You can use the things that would come against us to destroy and burn us and turn them around to release us and make our lives freer. In those circumstances, Holy Spirit please make me aware of Your presence with me and hold me close.
In Jesus Name, Amen.

3
Bowing Low

Where we have been...

Nebuchadnezzar builds an enormous statue and expects everyone to worship this idol. Daniel's friends, Shadrach, Meshach, and Abednego follow-through on their convictions to be faithful to God.

They were saved from the death sentence of a fiery furnace, imposed because they chose to stand tall when everyone else was bowing low. The Lord *is* my defender.

That story is a bold contrast to the one we are considering today. It is not a story of standing tall... but bowing low. In our culture bowing low in homage is not a usual practice, so stories around this practice can be uncomfortable. For example, I came across an example that I found very uncomfortable for me. It is when Daniel interpreted Nebuchadnezzar's dream of the statue, we are told the King responded by bowing down prostrate before Daniel.

Bible Reference
Daniel 2: 45-46

I don't think there is any way to read this, other than Daniel is being worshipped by Nebuchadnezzar. The king is bowing before him; he is making offerings and burning incense before him. It seems that this is more than a tribute of honour and respect. The King was unable to differentiate between Daniel and his God. To him, they are one and the same, and he is offering worship in what I understand is a very inappropriate way.

I think we have enough evidence to have confidence in Daniel's character, that his eyes were firmly fixed towards God.

I came across a familiar bible story, but it was told from a different the perspective...
It is the story of a donkey that is walking into a city... and the people gathered around that donkey calling out praises, and laying their robes on the ground for the donkey to walk over, and waving palm branches before his presence as he walked through the crowds...
Imagine the impact this could make on an impressionable, young donkey. How important would he feel to be acknowledged in this way! How inspiring and uplifting to be given such adoration!
There is only one way a donkey could walk through those crowds who were offering such accolades and praises, without his humility turning to pride. That is by acknowledging that the praises were not directed to him at all, but to the one he was in service to.
The donkey was in service to the son of God. The praises were for Jesus... who rode on his back. He was just the donkey.

Daniel was just the donkey. He was in service to the Most High God and in that way, he didn't make the mistake in thinking that the worship was for him. We can have confidence in Daniel's humble character and integrity... and his faithfulness towards God. He was able to direct and deflect the honour towards God. Daniel told Nebuchadnezzar it was the Great God who revealed the dream and its meaning, but it seems the King was unable to understand that. He revered the donkey, rather than the Holy One he was in service to... the Holy One, who truly held all authority over mysteries, dreams and interpretations. It is this tension between pride and humility that we are exploring as we continue to open the pages of another the story in the account of Daniel...

Bible Reading
Daniel 4:1-19

This account is written by the hand of the main character in this story: Emperor of the Babylonian empire, King Nebuchadnezzar.

For a long time, I hadn't realised that King Nebuchadnezzar wrote some of our scripture: isn't that a curious idea? The conquering heathen king of a Gentile world power had a revelation so powerful that God would include it in our Holy Scripture. Nebuchadnezzar's Empire is gone. His achievements are reduced to pieces of archaeology. But *this* revelation has been preserved and has endured for us... even today.

What is it like to notice that a Babylonian king wrote some of the bible?

Where have I excluded some people from being able to impart truth because of their past or their reputation?

The Dream held a message

This is not the first time Nebuchadnezzar has had a prophetic dream. He doesn't attribute them to God or the Holy Spirit. He is just disturbed by them. Yet there is something that he undeniably acknowledges: This dream had a message. It was telling him something... and it was something important.

The Meaning was Hidden

But the meaning of this dream, even though he knew it was significant, was hidden from him. Remember the dream of the tall statue? A statue was made up of many different compounds... gold, silver, bronze... right down to feet of iron and clay.

Now he has another dream. This time, not of a tall imposing statue... but of a tall imposing tree. And he doesn't understand it.

He has gone from being content and prosperous to afraid and terrified... because of this dream that he doesn't understand.

There are certain things he can decipher: he understands he tree has authority; the tree has power to offer protection; the tree is strong and abundant and has influence. But the rest is obscured.

First, he calls in his spiritual magicians and advisors. These are practitioners in deep occult practices. However, they are equally perplexed. Whatever they offer does not satisfy the king.

So, he calls in Daniel. He knows Daniel has the spiritual gifting and authority to interpret dreams. It seems odd that to me that Daniel is called in as a last resort. However, Nebuchadnezzar is desperate to get to the bottom of it... and he believes Daniel has the keys to unlock this mystery.

Interpreted to motivate change

I notice that Daniel is also terrified and perplexed. Not by the unknown... but by what was revealed! Perhaps he feels caught – condemned if doesn't tell the meaning (that's happened before), or condemned if he does explain it... because this is not good news!

But Nebuchadnezzar assures him of his mercy. He just wants to get to the bottom of it and he reassures Daniel he will execute him for telling the truth. So, Daniel tells him the interpretation.

What Daniel says, is not just an explanation... but it is a warning... an urging towards change. Appropriate action would change the trajectory of this dream. Repentance and aligning with God, could and would change the outcome of what was sent as a supernatural message of what was going to happen.

Bible Reading
Daniel 4:22-30

Daniel's warning goes unheeded. Instead... as time goes on, the serious caution of the dream fades, and King Nebuchadnezzar begins to feel indestructible.

"I am untouchable!"

He has lost his fear. He has lost the revelation of the God of Daniel who interprets dreams. He has lost the awareness of the awesome power of the God of Shadrach, Meshach and Abednego. His arrogance implants in him, a belief that he is untouchable. His greatness is like that tall, tall, magnificent tree that can be seen from all over the known civilised world... but he blots out the rest of the dream... and the warning.

Nebuchadnezzar literarily had everything: position, wealth, influence, success... yet he missed one important thing. Where have I gone looking for the success... and missed the important thing?

"I have accomplished!"

Not only was he great, but Nebuchadnezzar now declares that he alone was responsible for these accomplishments. The remarkable achievements of his life, the head of gold, was truly magnificent! The accumulated wealth and prosperity of his empire was his incredible legacy! This is true: the Empire of the Babylonians was extraordinary! But he made the error in claiming that *he* did it all. Uno. Solo. Alone. Single-handedly. No acknowledgement given to his advisors, his generals, his subjects, his workforce. No credit given to God.

Where am I inclined to honour my own resourcefulness and hard work, rather than the sovereignty of God?

"I glorify me!"

And right here we see the next step... it is the step that sends him over the abyss: *"by my mighty power and for the glory of my majesty!* I will give glory and honour to *me."* King Nebuchadnezzar goes from defending the God of Daniel and making decrees to honour the God of Shadrach, Meshach and Abednego to declaring that it was his own 'self' who had accomplished all this. He worships self; he gives glory and honour and honour to self. This is the creed, "I will worship me as my own god. I will pay tribute to me as my god."

Where has my pride not given acknowledgement to God for success?

This is post-modernism in an ancient pre-modern world. It is saying that every answer is within me. It is saying that I have control over my own destiny to the exclusion of all other influences. It is saying... as Eve declared in the Garden: God is not reliable. I will do it myself. "By my mighty power and for the glory of my majesty. I am that good." And then, even as Nebuchadnezzar makes this internal declaration, God speaks:

Bible Reading
Daniel 4:31-37

Nebuchadnezzar bows low by acknowledging...

God's Sovereignty

I am not going to suggest that mental illness is God's judgement on people's mistakes. Please don't take that away from this story. Yet in this instance, Nebuchadnezzar knows that the two are linked. He hears the voice of God. He knows it is God. He knows that God had removed his royal authority away from him. This happened, in his experience, by divine decree.

Nebuchadnezzar has a psychotic break with reality. In mental illness terms, this is the very rare and serious psychological disorder that has been documented, called boanthropy [pronounced *bowen-throw-pee*].

It is a condition where the person believes and behaves as if they are a cow or an ox. They eat grass as a cow. They live in the paddocks as a cow. This is a tragic situation where Nebuchadnezzar was brought to his knees. Most commentators agree that the "7-times", refers to not just a season, but literal years, so this happened for a significant period in his life: 7 years.

He was brought to a place of bowing low. By Nebuchadnezzar's own declaration, at the end of this time, he acknowledges that what happened did occur under the sovereign authority of God. He pens these words himself. This is not someone else imposing their ideas on him, but Nebuchadnezzar is sharing his own revelation.

Is there a word of caution I can take from this story?

What might be the consequences of brushing that aside?

God's Power

I have no doubt, that during this time, Daniel was praying for his king. Praying for healing and restoration. Praying that he would turn towards God, rather than turning away.

Nebuchadnezzar is healed. His healing came with the acknowledgement of God's sovereignty and power. God's authority to elevate, and to humble. His power to restore. His power to heal.

This would have to be the world's most remarkable come-back story. It is almost impossible in human terms, to be out of the picture for seven years, and then to be restored to the throne of a global empire. This is completely remarkable in the light of political ambitions, positioning and jostling. Yet incredibly, after this serious and extended episode of mental illness, Nebuchadnezzar is restored to his throne and his Kingdom. In politics... that doesn't usually happen. A gap in power is usually quickly filled by the next ambitious person.

Yet God determined it would be, and so he was restored, not just in his mind, but in his role. When God says he has the authority to elevate and humble rulers and dynasties, he really means it. This wasn't just an alignment of circumstances; this was the direct positioning of God. He can remove... and he can restore.

Once Nebuchadnezzar aligned with God and put himself in God's picture, rather than creating a picture that excluded God, then once again he was given insight and was able to acknowledge his place under the power and authority of God.

What gets in the way of praying for those who are afflicted, for their healing and restoration... and turning back towards God?

God's Glory

Then we see Nebuchadnezzar giving worship and honour and glory to God. Now he understands that there was nothing that he could hold in his hand. He could not hold onto the dream of a magnificent statue with a golden head and translate that into an actual imposing golden statue. He could not hold onto a dream of a grand tree, tall and strong, with abundant fruit. He could not even compare all the glories and wonders the of the Babylonian Empire to the glory and majesty of God.

Nebuchadnezzar bows low... this time, not through the humbling of psychosis, but through a heart that has been to hell and back, and understands humility is the first ground of greatness. Regardless of how great we are... perceived or recognised... first and foremost, it is God's glory and his greatness that is to be acknowledged.

He came to understand, regardless of who we are... we are just the donkey, in service that the greatest of Kings. Nebuchadnezzar's pride did not have the last say, his affluence, his success, his wealth and his prosperity did not have the last say. His advisors and armies did not have the last say. Mental illness did not have the last say. God did.

What inspires or challenges you in the idea that "humility is the first ground of greatness"?

When have you been tempted to believe the focus is all on you, when in fact you have been the donkey carrying the master?

Final thoughts...

Alex Haley, the author of the epic novel 'Roots', had a picture hanging in his office[iii]; it was of a turtle sitting on top of a fencepost. Alex says the picture is there to remind him of an insight he had long ago: 'If you see a turtle on a fence post, you know he had some help.' Alex says he is reminded that, "Any time I start thinking, 'Wow, isn't this marvellous what I've done!' I look at that picture and remember how this turtle, (me), got up on that post."

This is a healthy way of looking at achievement: acknowledging that regardless of whatever our fencepost is, we have had help to get there. It might be that other people in our lives have contributed. It might be *those who have mentored, and discipled, and taught us. It definitely is the grace and mercy of the God of heaven, because, in the words of King Nebuchadnezzar, "Everything he does is right, and all his ways are just. Those who walk in pride, he is able to humble.... The Most High is sovereign over all the kingdoms... all achievements on earth... and he gives them to anyone he wishes."*

There is a strong contrast in this story to the one about Shadrach, Meshach and Abednego where they stood tall... and they stood out... to honour God. This particular story is written by King Nebuchadnezzar's own hand. He was already standing tall, and he learnt how to humbly bow low. Nebuchadnezzar was learning that life is not intended to be ego-centric but centred around the honour and worship of God. Nebuchadnezzar's positioning and authority was not actually about him. The message of the dream was of a tree that provided protection, and provision, and a safe place. That was who Nebuchadnezzar was called to be: one who extends protection and provision and advantage to the people in his circle of influence. It was never intended that he set himself up as a god, or worship himself as if he accomplished those things by himself. Rather he was a turtle on a fence post, given that position through the generous positioning of the Most High and many unacknowledged people around him. The dream was a message about God's sovereignty and power and glory.

Nebuchadnezzar talks about the fear and terror he encounters when in his dream, that magnificent tree is chopped down. He knows this dream means something significant. Yet even after Daniel interprets the dream through the Holy Spirit, King Nebuchadnezzar does not heed its caution. Instead, he falls into a way of thinking where he takes all of the credit, all of the honour, all of the glory for himself. Suddenly he finds himself encountering a direct word of God... and all that it is taken all away... and he is humbled.

It is only as he acknowledges God's sovereignty, and acknowledges God's power, and acknowledges God's glory... and gives God worship and honour that is due, that he is restored, and given capacity to step back into the place God had called him to once more.

Prayer:

Father God, I acknowledge that you are my sovereign King. You hold all power, all authority. I give you honour and glory and worship your Holy Name as the Most High God. Thank you for surrounding me with people who have helped me up onto my own particular fencepost. Help me to remember to humbly acknowledge I am not created to be solo in this life. You have given me all sorts of people, gifts and opportunities, and to serve you is my purpose and privilege. Holy Spirit, increase my capacity to always to deflect honour to your worthy Name, because I am just the donkey and without you, I can do nothing.

4
Numbered Weighed and Measured

Where we have been...

As we turn the pages through the life of Daniel, we are discovering how to live well in our relationship with God, despite what is going on around us. We have seen how God gives us the capacity to not only stand tall, but to humbly acknowledge God's sovereignty by bowing low. The account written by the hand of King Nebuchadnezzar writes down this revelation in his own words. He gives praise, exalts and glorifies God the King of heaven, because "everything he does is right and all his ways are just. Those who walk in pride he is able to humble."

There is an old story of an Egyptian evangelist who met with one of the men in his discipleship circle, who had been a Muslim and recently gave his life to follow Jesus. He was a very educated man. The evangelist was curious as to what made the difference for this very articulate and analytical person to become a Christian, so he asked him, "What exactly shone truth on your way of seeing things? Which argument turned you around to follow Jesus?"

And the Egyptian answered this, "Every argument you presented I could refute, at least to my satisfaction.... But I could not refute your life. It was your life that convinced me."

Sometimes we can be passionate about the argument... but in the process forget that everything we do is being weighed and measured. This measuring is done using a different set of scales... scales of fairness, and kindness, and generosity.

The evangelist thought it was his clever apologetics and reasoning that made the difference, but in actual fact, it was the way he lived his life. His integrity spoke louder than his arguments.

The next story we consider looks at the idea that it is not only those around us who are looking for lasting and authentic worth, but it is also something that God is looking for.

Some background...

So, the account of Daniel has gone from the glory of King Nebuchadnezzar's empire, and then immediately we are in the court of a King Belshazzar. How does King Belshazzar fit into Daniel's experience?

Major Prophetic Literature

It is probably worth noting that the book of Daniel is not a chronological account of everything that happened in his life.

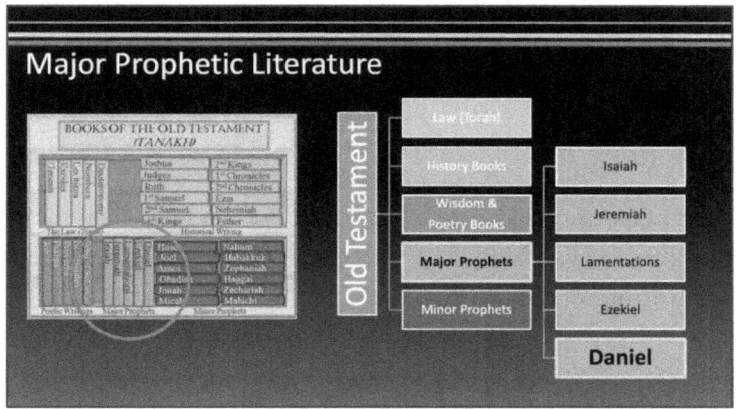

Daniel's position in the Bible library of books, is in the section of the Major Prophets, not History. Its primary purpose is its prophetic content. Daniel records a series of dreams and revelations that spoke about the greatness and sovereignty of God.

So, we go from an account set in the glory of King Nebuchadnezzar's Empire. Then in the next account we are immediately in the court of a King Belshazzar.

Historically there has been a lot of political change, intrigue, military coups and assassinations that occurred in between the end of Chapter 4 and the beginning of Chapter 5.

Even though we can take the message of Daniel without the history, I find it helps me to understand some of this context. So, who were the kings between Chapter 4 and Chapter 5? Was it simply a matter that King Belshazzar was next in line as Nebuchadnezzar's son?

For 43 years Babylon was under the reign of King Nebuchadnezzar. When King Nebuchadnezzar died, his son, King Awel Marduk came to the throne. He was also known as Evil-Merodach and is referred to in 2 Kings 25:27.

Bible Reference
2 Kings 25:27-30

Awel-Marduk was assassinated by his brother-in-law, Neriglissar who took the throne. King Neriglissar only had a short reign. After 4 years, he was also assassinated.

Then King Neriglissar's son Labashi-Marduk was crowned as a child-king. And he was assassinated nine months later.

1. **King Nebuchadnezzar:**
   Reigned 43 years

2. **King Awel-Marduk:**

   AKA "Evil-Merodach"

   Nebuchadnezzar's son

   Assassinated.

3. **King Neriglissar:**

   Assassinated

4. **Labashi-Marduk:**
   A child king.

   Assassinated

5. **King Nabonidus:**

   Military usurper.

   AKA - *'The absent king'* in exile.

   Married Nitocris – Nebuchadnezzar's daughter ("The Queen")

6. **King Belshazzar:**

   Reigning Prince Regent

   Nebuchadnezzar's grandson

The next King to take the throne was a Military usurper. Nabonidus was not related to King Nebuchadnezzar, but he may have married King Nebuchadnezzar's daughter Nitocris who is probably the "The Queen" referred to in Daniel 5:10. This King Nabonidus was known as 'The absent king" – because lived away from Babylon ten out of his seventeen-year reign, in fear of his life.

Finally, we get to King Belshazzar, where Daniel talks about him hosting this extravagant feast. He is the son of Nabonidus and was appointed as the reigning Prince Regent while his father was either out on military conquests or hiding for his life.

Both Nabonidus and Belshazzar held royal authority. Because Nabonidus married Nebuchadnezzar's daughter, technically Belshazzar was Nebuchadnezzar's grandson. Belshazzar apparently only reigned a couple of years. For many years there were critics who claimed this story out of Daniel was made up, because there was no external evidence of a Babylonian sovereign called King Belshazzar. However, as more archaeological evidence comes to light, we know that Belshazzar did exist[iv], and the details in this story are legitimate.

About five times in this account, it declares that Belshazzar was Nebuchadnezzar's *son*. It is assumed that this was a traditional designation of succession, similar to the way the prophet Elisha referred to Elijah as his father, even though there was no direct linage. It may have also been a way to claim his royal linage through his mother… giving legitimacy to his royal position.

So, between chapters 4 and 5 in the book of Daniel, we skip the reigns of four kings. That's a lot of political turmoil, conspiracies, instability and maneuvering that has taken place.

Daniel still holds a position within the court, but he is no longer holding a high profile. He is just getting on and doing his job.

Bible Reading
Daniel 5:1-4

Arrogance

The king is hosting an extravagant banquet. Over a thousand noble delegates and their attached entourages attend. During this banquet, they openly worship and praise their gods of gold and silver, of bronze, iron, wood and stone. This opulent, excessive banquet is an arrogant display of Belshazzar's power. Belshazzar parades to all his aristocrats, nobles and subjects... his influence, his authority to evoke indulgence, his wealth, and his dominion.

What measures do I use for success? Position? Wealth? Influence? Opinions? Something else?

And then, in an act of profound blasphemy, Belshazzar orders that the golden goblets that had been seized from the Hebrew temple be brought out. These items had been in the royal treasury, perhaps on display in a museum of sorts, for five generations of kings.

Bible Reference
Daniel 1:2

There is no ignorance in such an act. Something that was sacred, used in worship to the supreme God, was dismissed and treated as common, relative[v], usual. These articles of worship had been displayed alongside other spoils of war, other 'treasures'... just one of many. The underlying idea here is that there are no absolute or supreme truths, but everything is relative, even common and usual.

Where do I see precious absolute truths being misused as common and usual?

These goblets were taken out to serve in a drunken orgy. And this act closes, not just the chapter of Belshazzar's reign, but the collapse of the Babylonian Empire.

Bible Reading
Daniel 5:5-16

Defiance

Suddenly this orgy is interrupted with a message supernaturally written on the wall, and the whole event is shut down in a moment.

A hand appears and writes something on the wall. Everyone – it seems, can see the hand... and when the hand is gone, the inscription remains for everyone to scrutinise. There is such an upheaval with such a racket created, that the queen, who wasn't at the event, comes to investigate.

King Belshazzar has no understanding or capacity to interpret the inscription. He does not recognise the God of Nebuchadnezzar or acknowledge the weighty revelation that he had. He defiantly disregards the lesson learnt from King Nebuchadnezzar.

Ignorance

Belshazzar sees this miraculous inscription and he freaks out... as you would! He offers a reward to the man who could read it and interpret it. He offers the incentive of being appointed as the *third*-highest ruler in the kingdom – which would make sense, since we understand he was the reigning prince-regent, co-ruling with his exiled father. This is the highest available honour in the kingdom. He can't do better than this. The rewards that he offers are in line with the things that he values: Power, Wealth, Authority, A life of indulgence.

This is a situation where the king understands there are gaps in what he knows. He is aware of his ignorance. He calls on his advisors and magicians. Everyone and anyone is called up. But no one knows how to make sense of the message; no one knows the interpretation.

One bible resource suggests the written language was Samaritan Hebrew or Phoenician [vi] – and would be unknown to Babylonian scholars. Others believe that individually the text could be read, but the words didn't make sense.

Then the Queen – his mother, who was perhaps King Nebuchadnezzar's daughter, remembers Daniel, and comes forward. She would have known of her father's dreams. She would have known of her father's revelation and the decrees about honouring the God of Daniel. She would have been familiar with the miraculous stories of Shadrach, Meshach and Abednego. The Queen assumes that knowing the meaning of the message is enough to soothe her son's panic, and she recommends that Daniel be summoned.

But this message is not a soothing message.

Bible Reading
Daniel 5:17-31

God holds you in his Hand

King Belshazzar summons Daniel. Daniel gives very straight reasons why this message was delivered in this way. He makes it clear that God's wisdom is not a competition to be rewarded or a service to be bought. He tells the king he can keep all of his incentives and rewards. The things that the king esteems is not worth much to Daniel.

Daniel tells the king that the hand which wrote the message was sent from God. This wasn't a drunken or drug induced hallucination; it was a prophetic spiritual event. It was a visual aid, showing him that the divine God holds his life and all his ways in His hand.

For Daniel, being held in God's hand is a comforting idea. But for the King, in this situation, it is a horrifying word of correction. Daniel gives a very straight warning as to why this message was sent.

Is it a comfort to consider that God holds me sovereignly in his hand... or am I fearful of what he might not find?

Bible Reference
Daniel 5:22

Daniel immediately shuts down the idea of ignorance as an excuse. Belshazzar couldn't claim he didn't know. Ignorance is no defence of the law; especially when he "knew all this". Belshazzar did know about the stories, and he did know what had happened, and he had disregarded it anyway, and carried on in defiance without any respect or honour given towards God.

The interpretation Daniel offers, is that the King was not only aware that he is without excuse, but also that his arrogance has not gone unnoticed. Daniel gives a very straight interpretation. Some consider that the words were written in Aramaic, and were names of actual measures of currency:

MENE, a mina – this is a unit of currency that we are told was worth a hundred sheep. The word comes from the root meaning "to count".

TEKEL, was a spelling of 'shekel' – which is a unit of weight. This word comes from the root meaning "to weigh". It takes 60 shekels to make a mina... so we are going down in value, as the message progresses.

PERES, is half a mina. The word comes from the root meaning "to divide". It is also noticed that this word also resembles the word for "Persia", so there is a wordplay that is also happening on the wall.

So, if the message was read out literally as the names for weights and measures, the inscription is quite meaningless:
MENE, MENE, TEKEL, PARSIN: *"two minas, a shekel and two parts"*.

The interpretation that Daniel decrypts from these words is based on the passive verbs corresponding to the measurement names: *"numbered, weighed, divided."*

Numbered

MENE, MENE (Remember, from the root meaning "to count"). "God has numbered the days of your reign and brought it to an end." Daniel is affirming that God is the true sovereign judge.

What does God count and number in our lives?

God is the one who sovereignly determines then length our life. He numbers the hairs on our head. He numbers the days we live, the reigns of kings... or any position. The numbers the breaths that we breathe in our lives.

Weighed

TEKEL, (from the root meaning "to weigh"). "You have been weighed on the scales and found wanting." Daniel is affirming that God is not just the sovereign judge, He is also the just judge. God is the one who justly determines the weight or value that is lasting in our life. The picture of justice that we use in our court system is a lady holding balanced scales, calibrated and fair.

What would God weigh on his scales that he found wanting?

The weight of our deeds. The weight of our response to justice. The weight of our responsiveness to obligations in any position. The weight of love demonstrated in our life.

Divided

PARSIN, half a mina (from the root meaning "to divide"), but we have also noted that curious wordplay as it resembles the word for "Persia"). Belshazzar's kingdom was divided and given to the Medes and Persians. Daniel is affirming that God is the sovereign judge, the *just* judge and the allocating judge. God is the one who allocates the resources in our life. He distributed to Belshazzar a kingdom of great wealth, a role of great influence, and a position of great power. And he squandered the lot.

What things might God divide when someone is found wanting?

Belshazzar was not a good steward of those things placed in his hand. So, God took it, divided it and distributed it elsewhere. The account says "that very night" his palace was invaded, and he was executed. The age of the Babylonian Empire closes in one night and was taken over by the Darius the Mede.

Some final thoughts...

This is a sober story about King Belshazzar witnessing the writing of a sober message on the wall. In this story it is recognised that the King was given a lot and held many privileges and opportunities in his hand: Power, Wealth, Authority. He arrogantly took it all for granted and did not steward those opportunities well. What a difference it would have made if King Belshazzar understood that God is his judge, his Shophet. God held him in his hand.

What looks successful, God measures as a failure.
What looks influential and powerful, God weighs as unworthy.
What looks enduring, ends up divided, dismembered and swallowed up by another kingdom.

A Mother shares the story[vii] of driving while her high school daughter was sitting in the backseat with her friend. As the two girls chatted away, the mother enjoyed listening to their conversation from the front seat.
Her daughter spoke about a conversation that she had with her father a few weeks before he died. They were riding in his truck together. Just the two of them. She was sitting in the passenger seat talking with her dad when he began a conversation that she said was hard for her to hear. Whatever that conversation was, as this dad was talking with his daughter, she responded, and said, "Oh Dad, this is hard to hear!"
And then she said her dad reached over and held out his hand: "Here," he said. "Hold my hand." and for the rest of the conversation, he held her hand in his.
Can you picture this father reaching over to the passenger seat, offering his big, calloused hand and closing it around his daughter's soft, tender hand? Dad and daughter. Wisdom and inexperience. Protector and protected. Provider and recipient. Father and beloved.
Her father didn't stop the conversation. He didn't steer her around all of the hard words. She still had to listen to what he needed to tell her. But the entire time, he held her tight in his hand. And that made all the difference.
This mother finishes by saying "This is like our Heavenly Father. As believers, we don't get a pass on suffering. There will be hard things.

We will have to walk through them. And we are apt to cry out, "Oh, Father, this is too hard!"
God may not stop all of the hard, but He holds us tight in the palm of His hand."

Even though King Belshazzar had everything that looked successful, when the things in his life were numbered and weighed, he came up short.

In contrast to King Belshazzar, we notice the presence of Daniel, who understood that God was his defender – his Shophet, he humbly got on with his job regardless of the drama and intrigue around him. He understood that through the hard aspects of his life, God was there... a good father who held him in his hand.

Daniel was a person who stewarded what God placed in his hand well. Over the years, Daniel's life has been numbered, weighed and measured... and he has been shown over and over that his was a life well lived.

We all know the saying: "the writing is on the wall", meaning that a message of pending destruction is inevitable. The origin of that saying is literally from this story, when God delivered a message as God the Judge: A Shophet who also administers justice. King Belshazzar was not willing to acknowledge God's sovereignty and his accountability to him. He never acknowledged God's power. He never acknowledged God's glory, and he never gave God worship and honour that is his due. For him, it was horrifying to be held in God's hand under those circumstances.

Daniel always acknowledged God's sovereignty and was accountable to him. He always acknowledged God's power. He always acknowledged

God's glory, and he always gave God worship and honour that is his due. And it was a *comfort* for him to be held safely in God's hand.

Am I hearing a message of condemnation or a message of comfort?

The writing on the wall is a message about God holding us in his hand. God is the one who numbers, weighs and divides. This can be a message of fear and of condemnation. Or... it can be a message of comfort and reassurance. Reassurance that God is sovereign. God gets the last word. God is a carrier of mercy *and* justice. He holds each one of these dimensions, perfectly in balance in his hand. He holds us in his hand.

Prayer:

Father God, I thank you that you are our Shophet, our defender, our judge, the One who fights for us. You hold justice, and mercy and accountability in your hands in complete balance, just as you hold us in your hand. Holy Spirit, as I have reflected on this story and its sober message, I ask that you keep us mindful of our obligations towards You as our King, and we stand in service to You. Help us today to walk in dignity, humility and with integrity in the things you have given us to responsibly steward. May our lives be the louder message than any argument, or reasoning engagement that might be presented.
In Jesus' Name, Amen

5

Sitting with Lions

Where we have been...

We are discovering Daniel was a person who knew how to live well in his relationship with God, despite what is going on around him...

We've been mindful that Daniel's name means "The Lord is my Judge"; not the magistrate judge, but the Hebrew judge: "Shophet" who was anointed by God to deliver, defend and to fight and shield people from their oppressors. We have seen how God gives his people capacity to not only stand tall, but to humbly acknowledge God's sovereignty by bowing low and humbly steward what he gives them to do. We have also had the sobering reminder that if we don't engage with these ideas responsibly our life might be numbered, weighed and divided, like the caution given in the account of King Belshazzar. His arrogance would not acknowledge God's sovereign positioning.

Now we come to the most famous events of Daniel's life... where he spends a night sitting with lions...

I was listening to someone describe how they had been stuck in a massive traffic jam... on a major arterial highway. Traffic was backed up for miles and miles. The vehicles were not even edging forward. It was at a complete stand-still. For hours. I guess this is why that section of the highway is known as 'The Car Park'. As this person was talking, he described how his demeanour escalated from frustration to rage. He was powerless to change what was happening, and all he could do was sit in his car... and seethe for hours.

As I was listening to him recount his experience, he was still smarting from that horrible situation. My naturally empathetic self was feeling a little sympathetic for his plight. Then suddenly I realised something. I had been in that same traffic event! The dates, the time, the location and distance of the jam, were exactly the same. I had been there and experienced the same thing.

But my experience had been very different. We had food on the back seat... so we had a picnic. We called our daughter on the phone to join us on our virtual picnic, and we were able to talk and laugh with her without distraction. I can even remember saying after an hour or so... "Oh Darling... I'm so sorry but the traffic is moving again now..." It felt like an inconvenience that the traffic line was moving again and interrupting our time together.

Same event... we both had no control over the circumstances... but we did have control over the way we chose to experience what had happened.

There are many things that happen to us that are outside our control. It might be a benign as a traffic jam, or as serious as an extreme weather event... fire, flood, cyclones, or drought. It might be as disturbing as a grim medical diagnosis... or something as painful as a broken relationship.

Where is our focus at these times?

Bible Reading
Daniel 6:1-9

It Pleased the King

The Babylonian Empire was invaded by the Medes and Persians, and King Darius is now the new ruling sovereign. The account says nothing of the transition that Daniel goes through... but he is now a subject of the Empire of the Medes and Persians... and he has demonstrated that he will work for his new King: Darius the Great, just as diligently as he did under the Babylonians.

This part of Daniel's story begins with, "It pleased King Darius..." We are not reading about a democratic system. Ruling and laws are determined on the basis of what pleases the King. Appointments are made on what pleases the King. For those people who are wanting to progress within this system, it depends on the good-will and pleasure of the king. Within this system there are men who see themselves as Daniel's adversaries, the competition. They go about their own advancement by pleasing the king. They know the king is planning on making Daniel their boss, so they try to devise a way to discredit Daniel.

Trustworthy – pleases or problem

Daniel is not corrupted by bribes, nor does he fail by negligence. In every matter he is trustworthy. This quality of trustworthiness is noted. His peers note it. His subordinates note it. The King notes it. And it pleases the King.

Someone once told me that the true miracle in this story is that there is evidence of a clean, trustworthy, politician who was not corrupted.

Notice the two dimensions of this trustworthiness: He is not corrupted; and he was not negligent. King Darius thinks it would be a good thing for all his 'satraps' – the province governors, to be under the direct supervision of Daniel. Where the King considers Daniel's trustworthiness to be an asset to the wellbeing of his Kingdom, the other group notice that same characteristic... but in from their perspective this was a *big* problem. They are threatened and jealous of his qualities, his giftedness, his capacity... and plot to eliminate him.

Plots against his faith

The problem with plotting against someone who pleases the King, is that it must be done in a way that *'pleases the king'*! The major setback they come up against is that they can find no mud that will stick. Daniel is not corrupted with dodgy practice, nor dishonesty; he is not negligent, nor lacks diligence. He is exceptional in his work.

They decide that anything to discredit him had to be concerned with his faith in God. And right there, they go from opposing Daniel to declaring war against God. I notice that in their plots against Daniel, they are very careful not to mention Daniel's name. Ego is the primary factor they play to, as they go about trying to find a way to discredit Daniel. They make it all about how worthy the King is; how he deserves homage, honour and respect. Perhaps they sold this idea as an avenue to establish and embed King Darius' rule as the next great emperor of a global world power, in the vein and fame of Nebuchadnezzar. And King Darius, in his vanity, sets a new decree.

I can imagine how smug these rulers would have felt as the King confirmed the new law by pressing his signet ring and sealed this decree as law.

Bible Reading
Daniel 6:10-18

Daniel Recognises the Trap

The decree is published, and Daniel fully recognises that it is a trap. But he doesn't go to the King about the injustice of the decree. He simply carries on with his routine. Prayer... three times a day – "giving thanks to his God".

What do you think, in this situation, are the things Daniel found to give thanks for?

Yet he does. Thanksgiving three times a day. There is a political conspiracy against him. In his workplace there is gossip and scheming, and it seems there is no one whom he can seriously call his friend. And still, he gives thanks to God – first and foremost.

Am I so practiced at praise, worship and thanksgiving, that this becomes my go-to place?

Now Daniel adds to his prayer of thanksgiving by asking God for his help. Recognising the trap does not change what is good practice in his routine. It just means continuing to do what is already working... despite what is happening around him. Daniel sees nothing that needs adjusting or adapting. He heard the published decree... and his considered assessment is, keep on keeping on.

Am I a person who continues with my faith expressions even when others are offended by it?

The Law cannot be Repealed

Daniel hears the news, and nothing is changed for him. It is reported to King Darius that Daniel has been caught flouting the new decree. The King immediately recognises that *he* has been caught in a political agenda that had little to do with how worthy he was to received accolades and honour. Everything in the account indicates that Darius respects Daniel, or at least his work, but he is now in a situation where he has been deceived into making a decree against one whom he favoured.

The tradition of the Medes and the Persians was that once a rule was sealed with the King's seal, it became carved in stone, as it were. It could not be repealed. It could not be undone. No exceptions. To make a decree was a serious thing. Once made, people's lives were impacted; people lived and died accordingly. King Darius understands all of this in a moment of revelation and regrets his decision. He owns his mistake, but that doesn't help. He tries to find a loophole. He tries to find a way to extend mercy to Daniel, and to make him exempt from these consequences he had decreed. He realises that what he had made in a moment of vanity, now had consequences he regretted. Sometimes we can make decisions and there is no going back. There are some choices that we make that cannot be undone.

Daniel Relies on God for Results

So, what now? Is that the end? When we come up against consequences that seem to be spinning out of control, and they are not at all what we intended, and there are ripples that are beyond what we could ever anticipate... is that it? Do we end up being food for the lions? Perhaps... but perhaps not.

Daniel has already committed this outcome to God. Now Darius adds his voice to this prayer. He throws out a lifeline, begging Daniel's God for mercy, and relies on Him to amend the outcome of a really poor decision so that the results are changed.

Darius fasts all night. No food. No sleep. No entertainment. No visits from the harem.

Bible Reading
Daniel 6:19-28

Which Lion is dangerous?

One of the things that is remarkable about Daniel is his discernment. Which lion, which predator, is the problem in his situation?
Is it the giant cats that were in the den?
Is it the king, who made a vain and stupid law?
Is the political power of a world dominating superpower who worshiped the lion as a symbol of their strength?
Is it the scheming jealousy of his peers who want him eliminated?
Daniel knows, that to some degree... all four are dangerous. They all contributed to his position. After all a lion has four paws.

The Lions were Hungry but did not devour

Daniel knows that his position is vulnerable. He is not blasé or indifferent to his predicament. He knows that God is able to help and save him. Each of these four 'lions', contribute to his situation. But which one will devour him?

The Lions:

These giant cats were used to execute political prisoners for crimes against the empire and the emperor. Wild lions were locked up. They were kept hungry, starved, so that they would not hesitate to attack. They were kept agitated so that they were irritable and volatile. This was as deadly as any firing squad as a means of execution.

But the lions' hunger does not mean that Daniel is devoured. The God who created all things, even these powerful beasts, is his defender.

The King:

In a moment of vanity, King Darius is beguiled into making a blasphemous and imprudent decree. Yet Daniel does not blame him. The King's hunger for honour does not mean that Daniel is devoured. The God Most High, who rules over all, is Daniel's defender. It seems that God does not hold his blasphemy against the king either and listens to his prayer to save Daniel.

The Empire of the Medes and Persians

The insignia of the Empire of the Medes and Persians was a winged lion. Execution by being thrown into a Lions' Den is a statement of condemning a man for crimes of treason against the Empire. This sentence could be seen as a stand-off between the power of the Medes and Persians who worshiped the lion as a symbol of their strength, and the God who created the lion.

The creator and the created:

Yet Daniel understands that the power imbalance is not against him. The Sovereign God is his defender. With God on his case, he has the balance of power on his side.

The Scheming Peers:

Does their jealous agenda hold the power to eliminate Daniel? Daniel's crime was not just about defying the decree of State to bow down and pray only to the emperor as the official deity. What really offended his peers was that he held favour with the King. Daniel's integrity showed them up. His competence meant he would be promoted to a position higher than them. His trustworthy work would expose *their* lack of reliability. His honesty meant that there would be a leash put on their corruption. Yet Daniel doesn't point the finger, and he doesn't lay blame. He just reinforces his personal stance of faithfulness in service. He understands their hunger for power does not mean that Daniel is devoured. The faithfulness of God who is with him, is his defender.

God is my Defender

I wonder what it would be like to spend a night locked up with cranky, hungry, frustrated lions, who can see dinner but can't eat it because an angel has shut their mouths? Sometimes, I look at artists' impressions to get an idea of how they interpret a scene or a scripture. How do they imagine what it would be like... spending that night sitting with the lions?

*Daniel in the Lions' Den
by Sir P. P. Rubens; c. 1615*

*Daniel in the Lions' Den
by Siegfried Detler Bendixen
c. 1850*

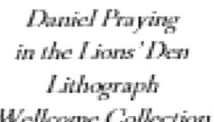

*Daniel Praying
in the Lions' Den
Lithograph
Wellcome Collection*

*Daniel Lion Den
by Ivan Garcia on DeviantArt*

*Daniel in the Lions' Den by Robert Edward Weaver,
c. 1952*

What about these paintings draw your attention?

As you can imagine, there are a lot of variations. One painting, by the classic Baroque master Rubens, has Daniel looking absolutely in a state of panic: terrified, clasping his hands in prayer pleading for deliverance. Another has Daniel snuggling up to the lions, cuddling them like a big, fluffy, soft toy. To me, there is something that is uncomfortable in both those extremes. I think one of my favourites is the stylised painting by Robert Edward Weaver. The lions' large eyes and hungry looks, goes unnoticed by Daniel, as he kneels serenely in prayer.

God is my Defender

I don't think for a minute that Daniel played with the lions and had games. He didn't make friends with them or use them as pillows. The angel didn't put the lions into a deep state of satisfied sleep... because when Daniel's accusers were executed for their political subterfuge, the account says that their bodies did not even reach the ground before they died. The lions were not a bit off colour. They were not suddenly tame. They were still wild. They were still agitated. They were still hungry. But they were powerless to touch Daniel, because God decreed it.

When Daniel talks to the king in the morning, he is composed and calm, and he is respectful. It suggests to me that Daniel, despite being in the most dangerous and vulnerable position, held a calm and a peace, through it all. So even through the danger, Daniel carries peace into the den and gets through the night, sitting with lions. Unhurt... not even a scratch. No panic attacks. Calmly aware of the angelic servants who were deployed by God on his behalf had kept him safe. Daniel was aware that God was defending with him through this dark night, sitting with the lions.

At daybreak Daniel is lifted out, because his sentence has been fulfilled. His sentence was that he was to be thrown into the den, not that he had to stay there and never come out. Daniel's escape could not be anything other an act of God.

This was not just an escape from death. It was also a declaration that God is bigger than the created; bigger than the lion; bigger than the emperor; bigger than the Empire; bigger than his disgruntled peers. The lions' mouths were shut. God is sovereign. These Lions were symbols of rulers who reigned with power and fear. Now King Darius issues a new decree... one that honours God... not himself.

What insights does King Darius have, as he rewrites the decree?

Final thoughts...

Daniel's night of sitting in the lions' den is a famous story. Even though it is one that we have probably heard many times, it is good to remind ourselves what it is about. It considers that there are sometimes unpleasant aspects of being a person of capacity and integrity and faith.

Daniel holds a position of influence, through many changes of rulers and kings, even empires. And some people don't like him... and the reason they dislike him is connected to him just getting on and doing his job to the best of his ability. When a trap is laid, Daniel recognises it for what it is, and even when there are decisions that are made outside his control... he throws himself... with thanksgiving... into the hand of God. God is his defender.

Even though there was many who contributed to the situation, Daniel never laid blame. He could have fallen into another trap – the trap of laying blame. Instead, he just continued in his life and work and faith expressions. Regardless.

When I come up against something that is outside my control... what do I do?

Do you identify with any of the following?

☐ *Spiral into anxiety and panic?*

☐ *Trying to snuggle up to the problem and try to make it my friend?*

☐ *Get caught up in a trap of laying blame?*

☐ *Notice my anxiety and fight for my internal peace?*

In 1555, Nicholas Ridley, the 'Bishop of London and Westminster' was sentenced to be burned at the stake, under Heresy Laws, during the time that was known as the Marian Persecutions in England. He was sentenced to death because he taught that the Christian communion elements were symbolic, and not actually transformed into the living flesh and blood of Jesus.

On the evening, before Ridley's execution, his brother offered to stay with him in his prison cell, to support and comfort him through the night. Nicholas declined the offer and said that he would just go to bed and get a good night's sleep, just as he normally would. That is what he did. He slept, and then in the morning, he faced his sentence with courage.

There is granite cross paved into the road outside one of the colleges of Oxford university, where he and a couple of his peers died that day. Today, what Ridley taught, is not controversial; it is accepted by protestants around the world as sound biblical teaching. God has defended his position.

Ridley was able to sleep during the night because he knew the peace of God. He could rest in the strength of being held in God's hand. He was thrown to the lions, yet he could trust that the peace of his Lord would stay with him to meet his need. I don't think Ridley's story is less victorious, just because the outcome was different. The way he faced his Lion's Den experience was with the same courage and peace shown by Daniel.

Ridley could not change the outcome of the decrees and issues he was fighting, in the political and religious landscape of his country, but he could do his part, and fight to hold onto the Peace of God in those circumstances... and leave the rest to God.

When Daniel was thrown into a dark den of danger, he relied on the presence of God where he was. The fight was not with the lions, nor the king, nor the Empire, nor his critics... but with his own internal peace. He fights for his peace, knowing that he is held in God's hand.

Daniel acknowledged it was God who is fighting for him. Just as Daniel's name suggests, God was his Shophet, his defender. He acknowledged and worshipped God's power and glory. He acknowledged God's mercy – even when the king was powerless to extend mercy. It was a comfort for him to be held safely in God's hand... even when sitting through the night with the lions.

Prayer:

Father God, thank you that you see all of our circumstances. You know when we have been falsely accused. You know when there are things that are happening outside our control, that are spinning in a direction that we had never anticipated. We ask Holy Spirit that you would help us discern what we are really fighting for. Help us to fight for that sense of being in your presence; to fight to retain our peace, and our internal sense of wellbeing. We thank you that you are our defender!
In Jesus Name, Amen.

6

Go your way

Where we have been...

All through our reflections on Daniel, we've been mindful that his name means "The Lord is my Judge". Not the magistrate judge, but the Hebrew judge: "Shophet" – those anointed by God to deliver, defend and to fight and shield people from their oppressors. God is that sort of judge in Daniel's life... and in our life as well. We have looked at the account where Daniel was set-up to defy a new law that was set in place to deliberately discredit him with King Darius. Daniel was sentenced to death by being thrown into a den of lions. An angel of the Lord shut the lions' mouths, and he was kept safe as he spent that night, sitting with lions. Daniel never laid blame but fought to retain his peace in a place that was not at all peaceful.

Chapter 6 marks the end of the accounts of Daniel that are written as narrative. The last half of the book is dedicated to the record of three primary prophetic visions that Daniel experienced starting from the time that King Belshazzar took the throne.

However, before we close the book of Daniel... I don't think we can finish considering his story, without looking at some of the prophetic visions that he was given, that he was told applied to "the times of the end", and how he responded to these incredible insights himself.

When I was a young child, I remember one night going to bed and not being able to sleep. In fact, I was so distressed that I was crying and having trouble breathing. I didn't have the language for it then, but now

I would understand that as an episode of high anxiety... or even a mild panic attack.
My mother came in and sat on my bed, and in her way, she was able to help me calm, and extract from me what was disturbing me. I had seen an item on the News broadcast that reported that Sydney was going to drown. That very night. They had the diagrams showing the rise of waters that would cover Sydney Harbour Bridge.
They had projections that showed how many suburbs would be inundated. In my child's-mind, if such devastation was going to cover Sydney and its famous landmarks, then even our little country town, which was nowhere near Sydney, would also be inundated, and in the morning, I would wake up to find that I had drowned during the night.
At that age, I did not give consideration to the fact there were no evacuation processes activated. All I knew was that a voice of authority had told me that Sydney Harbour Bridge was going under.
Nothing my mother told me, convinced me that this pending doom did not apply, if not to me, at least to thousands of other children who were going to bed, like I was in that moment, and they would 'wake up dead'.
In the end... the thing that allowed me to close my eyes, was... that Mum talked to me about what we can do, right now, in this moment... even if this happens. She told me to fight for my calm because we know that Jesus is with us. She told me that this was not the end of the world, and it probably wouldn't happen the way that they predicted this disaster to play out.
Over 50 years later... As far as I could determine, Sydney Harbour Bridge has never been inundated with rising harbour water.

There are a lot of voices that report disaster in our world. All of it is horrifying and distressing. Some of it is real; some of it is sensationalised; some of it is projected and fabricated. We have unregulated access to this type of media-hype that is designed as click-bait to generate a following, and views. One of these voices is the ongoing discussion around "End Times". It is important to maintain a balanced approach in the way we look at this subject. It is fairly easy to become weird and unbalanced about it, and to lose sight of God's sovereignty, and what our spirituality means as we do life here, now, where God has positioned us.

Daniel's visions:

There are libraries dedicated to the books exploring the interpretation of Daniel's incredible visions. We are not going to focus on the interpretation of these prophetic visions, but instead, look at the way that Daniel interacted with the privilege of being entrusted with these visions and insights. Perhaps we can use these reflections to find a way in which we can also interact with the subject of the End Times in an honourable and helpful way.

Bible Reading
Daniel 7:1-28

Time-stamped

One thing I notice about this vision is that it is time-stamped. It tells us when Daniel was given the vision. In the description of the vision, he is told when the content of the vision would occur and what it referred to. It is as if God takes Daniel by the hand and zooms out in history. He is not looking under a microscope at the detail of events, but he is given the wide panoramic view of the rise and fall of political and religious powers.

This vision was given to a man, who, in his lifetime, had served under at least seven kings of world-dominating empires. Different styles. Different agendas. Different loyalties. Yet even in his lifetime of service, God shows Daniel, that this is just a small part of the whole story of history. The things that are going to happen are not a surprise to God.

God's time for these matters is set and stamped. God knows when and where and who and how.

Terrifying

Another thing I notice, is that this vision blows Daniel's mind. It is a terrifying revelation! We don't usually think of Daniel in terms of experiencing anxiety and being so emotionally overwhelmed he not able to cope with what he experienced. After all, he could stay calm and together, all night in a den of agitated lions. Yet even the great hero Daniel... experienced overwhelm. This was too much!

What he was shown, was not just about the rise and fall of one man's story, but whole nations and empires and world powers. This is the newsreel of history in fast forward. And yet Daniel has no-where to take or share this vision. All he can do is to journal it and keep it to himself.

Notice that he doesn't jump onto social media and blog about his incredible experiences, insights, interpretations and timelines. He quietly absorbs his revelations... and it says... "he kept them to himself."

Turbulent times

The visions speak of turbulent times. There is no prosperity-tone to these prophetic visions and dreams. It is hard, it is traumatic, and it is global. And yet God allows Daniel to witness these things in all of its ugly power and oppression.

He gives Daniel an angelic guide to walk with him through understanding some of the interpretations of these visions. This is probably one of the hardest challenges when reading these visions. Where do I place my focus? On the imagery, on the events, the probable interpretation, or the layers of meaning? Do I allow myself to become so distressed about what they mean, that like Daniel I lose my appetite, I lose sleep, and become anxious? Or do I focus on the Ancient of Days, who manages all these things?

I have had various conversations with people who are deeply enmeshed in end-time eschatology and interpretations. I notice that they are very passionate about the subject, but the danger is that passion can become unbalanced and skews their thinking and perspectives. The end result can be high anxiety, dogma, or even judgemental, suspicion of every bear or lion or political leader who might be represented in these end-time visions.

So how do we discern or measure if something is off balance? Here are some questions to prompt your reflections:
Have I left a conversation feeling there is no hope left for mankind?
Have I noticed the conversation distracts from Jesus and his kingship?
Does it steer away from the Sovereignty and authority of God?

The truth is that God is in control. The truth is that God knows the end of the story. The truth is that God – the Ancient of Days... is moving history towards his predetermined point of redemption and hope... not pain and destruction.

The three most powerful and enduring fruits of God's spirit is FAITH, HOPE and LOVE. We must look towards things that build our faith that God is not only good... but sovereign and powerful. We must look towards things that anchor our hope that God is not only good... but faithful and trustworthy. We must look towards things that expand our capacity to love because our God first loved us... and he is also merciful and gracious.

There is no doubt that Daniel witnessed turbulence in his vision. Unprecedented turbulence. But he also witnessed God's sovereignty, and he also witnessed that these events are moving towards God's final ruling of redemption. What Daniel witnessed, was as clearly imparted as John on Patmos in his vision of Revelation. He also witnessed the return of Jesus to Earth to rule and reign, and to be worshiped and honoured. They both saw that regardless of the narrative that history appears to be writing, God – the Ancient of Days, sits sovereign on the throne, ruling with majesty and power with a more hopeful, loving and faith inspiring narrative.

What is our response when we hear of our own turbulent times through the media?

Are we confused as to how such pain and turbulence is possible? Do we become anxious and overwhelmed by the magnitude of evil? Or... do we allow, that although in many respects our world is getting better... and in other respects our world remains troubled and base and unredeemed.

When we hear these unredeemed stories... what can we do to remind ourselves that God already knows about it?

That means...
We are not too surprised... not really.
We are not too shocked... not really.
We know we have been given the heads-up.
We realise were told about this.
God is not a God of chaos...
His first act of creative genius was to move in the chaos and create order when he spoke creation into being. His final act of creation will be to restore order out of the chaos generated by sin. We know this, because, in the chaos that exists, God has already delivered a message of stability, calm, victory, peace and restoration. He has already imparted the vision.

Our God is not a God of hopelessness. But in the hopelessness of our world, he brings a message of hope and security and confidence that God has a plan of healing.

So, there will be turbulence... but there is also a plan of reinstating order and the shalom – the peace and wholeness, of God's redemptive presence.

There are always two parts to the visions:
The turbulent part;
And the part of God's restoration and salvation.

Why do you think we focus on the chaos and not more on God's plan for how the chaos will be redeemed?

In Daniel chapter 8 we'll read some selected verses of his next vision.

Bible Reading
Daniel 8: 1-5; 13-21; 26-27

Eschatology

Eschatology – concerns a distant future. Gabriel tells Daniel that this vision refers to "The Time of the End", that it concerns a distant future... what we dub "End times".
Eschatology – is the study of End Times from God's perspective. This is part of what Daniel is given insight into. His dreams are packaged with images and metaphors, to make it presentable to him.

This is a magnificent charge that the Holy Spirit entrusts to Daniel: large visions, insight, knowledge, understanding, and explanations. He tells Daniel that this particular vision concerns a distant future... a future that Daniel will never personally experience. God gives Gabriel the authority to name what the ram and the goat represent.

These represent political and military rulers, and their successors, that are progressively overpowered... but each reign was no less destructive.

End Times: "The Time of the End"

Scripture commentaries suggest we are in well and truly immersed in the end times. We understand that the time from Jesus' resurrection and ascension into heaven... until he returns again... is the "End Times". This is what the Christian calendar calls "The Age of The Church". This is what Peter spoke about at Pentecost when he spoke about the fulfillment of the they were baptised in the Holy Spirit.

Bible Reference
Isaiah 44:3; Zechariah 12:10
Acts 2:17

Peter is saying that "In the last days..." the fulfillment of the prophets was to be fulfilled. They were living that fulfilment on the day of Pentecost. That has already happened. That first Pentecost was a marker: The beginning of Last Days. This is what we celebrate at communion – the declaration that Jesus died, rose again and ascended into heaven... an acknowledgement that we are in 'The Last Days', 'The End Times', until Jesus returns again.

Gabriel specifically identified that the Goat in this vision refers to the Greek empire. Theologians who have studied this, refer to the sweeping influence of Alexander the Great. That powerful Greek King is still recognised as one of history's most formidable military generals. Alexander the Great would rise to power, two-centuries after Daniel's life, a distant future. Yet for us, that era of the Empire of Greece, well and truly falls into the 'Ancient history' section of our libraries. So... we can be sure, that God's timeline is running its course. What was revealed has come to pass.

Am I confident God's plan of redemption is on track? Why or why not?

Do we know the time frame when the rest of it will be finalised?
No. We do not.
It is recorded five times (Matthew 24:42; Matthew 25:13; Mark 13:33;35; Acts 1:7) by the writers of the gospels that Jesus himself spoke

to his disciples and said, you do not know on what day your Lord will come.

So... if Jesus has said very distinctly that we do not know, and not only that... specifically, it is not for us to know, then how much energy are we to spend on trying to work this out? Are we stepping into territory that is not ours to occupy in terms of time and energy?
Are there other priorities for us to be focussing on?

Exhausting

Daniel found this vision, and the effort of trying to understand it, exhausting. It physically depleted him. He was sick and appalled. He couldn't get out of bed for days. In today's terms, I would understand, that he was overwhelmed with anxiety. Eventually he made a decision, to get up and get on with life, and he went back to work, attending to the King's business. He set it aside and attended to the here and now.

Bible Reading
Daniel 9:1-23; 10:1-19; 12:2-13

Go your way...

Daniel was determined to acquire understanding. All of these incredible insights, started with a resolution by Daniel to understand more about the things of God. Daniel acknowledges that political take-overs and world affairs; the rise and fall of Emperors and Empires were not merely a secular matter, but were firmly in the domain of the divine. These are matters that were held in the hand of the Ancient of Days. And Daniel wanted to understand more.

I notice that Daniel was a man of prayer. He started his pursuit of understanding with prayer, confession and standing in the gap for his nation and his people. He devoted himself to intercede for a nation that seemed in such a state of disrepair, that they were unable to pray for itself.

Allotted time to pray

This account is a beautiful description of prayer.
Daniel seeks.   God responds.
Daniel asks.   God answers.
Daniel's prayer becomes a sacred conversation of trust. His pursuit of discernment and understanding is given layers of more insight. I also notice that Daniel records the visions as they were presented – without embellishment, without his own twist, slant, version or interpretation. He records the metaphors and images as they were shown to him. He documents the words of Gabriel, as they were spoken to him.

I would suggest that if this subject does not motivate us to become more committed to prayer, then something is out of balance. This topic is not intended to be fodder for circular discussion. For Daniel it was fodder for prayer.

Do I start, continue and conclude my exploration of End Times with confession, intercession and prayer?

Directed to "Go your way..."

What is the end of all this? Daniel didn't know what was expected of him now. What did this trust mean? What would be the conclusion to these incredible visions and insights that Daniel himself describes as "appalling; beyond understanding; astonishing."

The angelic messenger gives him a very specific directive: "Go your way." And then he repeats it: "Go your way." This suggests to me that Daniel might have been ready to stop... pause... quit... give up or give out. That his anxiety, his pale face, lack of appetite, was washing out his capacity to live fully.

What does it mean to me, that I will rise again and receive an allotted inheritance?

Where is God encouraging me to get on with the life that he has called me to, where he has positioned me?

But the message is: don't give up. Keep going. Keep on keeping on.

Continue to be faithful in what God has called you to, because God is faithful. This is active waiting... not passive waiting. Keep making a difference where one is positioned. The plan for Daniel's life was still the same plan. God's plan for salvation and redemption is still the same plan.

Bible Reference
Daniel 12:13

Be the person God has created you to be. Continue to do the things, where God has positioned you, with integrity. Keep doing it well, just as you have been doing. And then at the resurrection of the God's people, Daniel will rise to receive his allotted inheritance. The plan for Daniel's life was still the same plan. It had not changed.

The plan for our life is still the same plan. It has not changed. Our resurrection has always been part of God's design of salvation.

Even Daniel needed to yield to the idea that this world is imperfect. Its history was imperfect and filled with pain. Its future will be imperfect and filled with pain. Its kings, governors and rulers will be imperfect and perpetrators of pain.

In the words of Gabriel, God's messenger, "the wicked will continue to be wicked". Just because Daniel was given a preview of history, those insights didn't change the trajectory of the outcome of it all.

Regardless of the revelations of evil and profound powerful angelic forces, God plan of salvation is still moving towards the redemption of mankind... and the redemption of creation.

The overarching reality of it all, and the underpinning certainty, is that God is in control. There is goodness and integrity and grace that is supervising the outcome. I wonder why there is a tendency to skip of Gabriel's observation that many will be purified, made spotless and refined? Even in a world full of evil... good people will continue to follow God's wisdom and live well... just as Daniel did.

Do I tend to focus on the terrifying political dynamics of the world around me... or am I drawn to the truth that all world events are held in the hands of the 'Ancient of Days' who continues to orchestrate good?

'Go your way'. You will rise. You will receive an allotted inheritance. That is an incredible promise! One that we can hold onto through all of the pain and chaos.

Some final thoughts...

Through the visions of Daniel, we get a glimpse of something that was beyond even Daniel's comprehension. It is a combination of terrifying political and secular and spiritual dynamics that are all held in the hand, and the plan, of the 'Ancient of Days' – the Almighty God.

Daniel is shown things that are for a distant future... the time of the end. Some of what Daniel was shown, we understand is already ancient history for us. Other things we believe, refer to the season we live in now, which is the Age of The Church... the time between Jesus' ascension... and his return and second coming.

In her memoir, "The Hiding Place," WWII Holocaust survivor, Corrie ten Boom, tells the story of a conversation she had with her father when she was a little girl. Corrie was seated next her father in the train compartment, and she had asked him a question about sex, something she had read about in a poem. Rather than answering her question directly, Corrie's father paused....
She writes this:

"He turned to look at me, as he always did when answering a question, but to my surprise he said nothing. At last, he stood up, lifted his traveling case off the rack and set it on the floor "Will you carry it off the train, Corrie?" he said.

I stood up and tugged at it. It was crammed with the watches and spare parts he had purchased that morning. "It's too heavy," I said. "Yes," he said, "and it would be a pretty poor father who would ask his little girl to carry such a load. It's the same way, Corrie, with knowledge. Some knowledge is too heavy for children. When you are older and stronger, you can bear it. For now, you must trust me to carry it for you."

"And I was satisfied," Corrie writes. "More than satisfied—wonderfully at peace. There were answers to this and all my hard questions — for now I was content to leave them in my father's keeping."

Sometimes, it is okay, even appropriate, to allow our questions to be 'a suitcase thing' and allow that our Heavenly father will carry that knowledge until we need to open that 'suitcase'... until we have the capacity to carry it, or until we need the contents of that suitcase for the next part of our journey.

Until then, we can be 'wonderfully at peace' knowing the answers are in our Father's keeping.

Daniel is a man of profound discernment and capability, and yet these revelations were even beyond him. This was a very heavy suitcase. In the other stories of his life, we've notice how Daniel continued on with what he needed to do. He continued faithfully in his life and faith expressions, regardless of the evil he was surrounded by. Daniel knew God was defending him. He knew God was in control. So many times, we have seen Daniel was comforted by the knowledge that he was held safely in God's hand... Defended by God's love.

This comfort also applied when there were profound and incomprehensible revelations and visions that were being unfolded for him. And even though Daniel asked for these revelations and insights, he found the contents of this suitcase was very heavy. Too heavy for him to carry. In the end he had to repack that suitcase, and let God carry it for him. That way Daniel was able to continue on in his call, and his life work, because of his confidence that God, his father, carried this suitcase and is faithful to his plan of salvation that is moving towards the redemption of creation.

Go your way. You will rise. You will receive an allotted inheritance.

That was Daniel's incredible promise. This is our promise also. 'God is my Defender' – the Ancient of Days is our Judge. He is our Shophet. He is our Defender. Our Heavenly Father graciously carries the suitcase that holds the answers to all of this. This is our comfort too. God carries this suitcase if we allow him to. God is our defender.

Prayer:

Father God, the Ancient of Day, Holy One. We praise you. We honour that you are the One who holds times, and places, and people, and empires, and kingdoms of the Earth in your hand. We thank you that you have a plan to redeem your creation. We know that this is a plan that is time-lined in your wisdom. And we know you have kept everything on track. Nothing happens by surprise, that you don't know about. Help us to rest in the confidence that you hold. This suitcase firmly in your hand. Holy Spirit, give us wisdom when we can unpack some of those things in that suitcase, and when we need to trust you are holding that for us, according to your timeline and plan. Give us strength and courage and integrity to continue to go our way, and to faithfully continue to do what you have called us to do where you have positioned us.

In Jesus Name, Amen.

Closing reflection...

As we close the book of Daniel... there's lots to consider, so let's pause before we look at some questions, which may help some of the wisdom in this book, to settle in our hearts.

I invite you to quietly reflect on what has been happening for you as we have talked about Daniel's life; the events, challenges, faithfulness and visions of end times. Are you feeling calm, anxious, worried, excited, defensive, bored, curious? See if you can notice what is happening for you ... and name it.

What do you notice?

Whatever we feel right now, is not right or wrong... it is just a way of understanding more of how we are interacting with this information.

Now I would invite you to turn your attention to be aware of the Holy Spirit with you. Be aware of his love, peace, kindness, gentleness, patience, faithfulness.
He is here.
He is our counsellor... the giver of wisdom. Notice his wisdom.
He is our comforter... the source of our wellbeing. Notice his peace.
He is our defender ... the protector of our lives. Notice his strength and security.

Other books in this Series

End Notes:

[i] *John Lennox – Against the Flow: the Inspiration of Daniel in a Time of Relativism – Presentation in Oslo, 2019.*

[ii] *https://sheridanvoysey.com/are-angels-real-stories/*

[iii] *https://www.sermonillustrations.com/a-z/h/humility.htm*

[iv] *https://biblearchaeologyreport.com/2024/01/19/belshazzar-an-archaeological-biography/*

[v] *John Lennox – Against the Flow: the Inspiration of Daniel in a Time of Relativism – Presentation in Oslo, 2019.*

[vi] *John Gill's Exposition of the Bible*

[vii] *https://lisaappelo.com/held-is-his-hand/*

[viii] *V0034351 Daniel praying in the lion's den. Lithograph.*

Credit: Wellcome Library, London. Wellcome Images images@wellcome.ac.uk http://wellcomeimages.org Daniel praying in the lion's den. Lithograph.

www.ingramcontent.com/pod-product-compliance
Lightning Source LLC
Chambersburg PA
CBHW052105070526
44584CB00017B/2348